THE CORRAL BARS ARE DOWN

WESTERN POEMS
A RODEO OF COWBOYS,
CATTLE, COYOTES AND CAYUSES

To Joan & Bill,
Enjoy your ride through
these pages! Wendy Vaughan

BY:
WENDY VAUGHAN

ILLUSTRATED BY:
GINA McDOUGALL-COHOE

September 2003.

National Library of Canada Cataloguing in Publication

Vaughan, Wendy, 1943-
The Corral Bars Are Down: Western Poems: A rodeo of cowboys, cattle, coyotes and cayuses / Wendy Vaughan; Gina McDougall-Cohoe, illustrator.

ISBN 0-9733710-0-5 bound
ISBN 0-9733710-1-3 soft cover

1. Cowboys—Poetry.
2. Ranch life—Poetry. I. Title.

PS8593.A954C67 2003 C811'.6 C2003-904713-X

Cover Sketch by
Gina McDougall-Cohoe

Cover designed by
Daran Fletcher

Published by Off the Beaten Path Marketing Inc.
R.R. #2
Crossfield, Alberta, Canada
T0M 0S0

Printed and bound in Canada by Friesens Corporation

First Edition
Manufactured in Canada.

Contents

Page

Dedication

This book is dedicated to:

The memory of Mum and Dad,
Tillie and Jim Richards,
whose lifestyle provided the inspiration and material for
many of the poems in this book.

And also to:

My husband, Walter, and daughters, Alberta and Amanda
who have put up with years of me
writing and reciting poetry.

Foreword

When she's not involved with farm animals, office work, or just plain keeping track of the family (husband Walter and daughters, Alberta Rose and Amanda), Wendy Vaughan's indelible memories come to life and her mind works double time pursuing a pastime she lives and loves, composing and writing poems - relating to true-life happenings from the foothills of Alberta's cattle country - now captured in: "The Corral Bars are Down."

A cherished longtime friendship between Wendy and illustrator Gina McDougall-Cohoe, famed Western Artist and Bronze Sculptor, began in 1946 when Wendy was just three years old, living with her parents, Jim and Tillie Richards, and younger brother, Doug, on the family homestead on the south side of the Ghost River, bordering the Nakota Nation (our Stoney Indians). The neighbouring Bar C Ranch, on the north side of the Ghost, was home to Gina Southern, a young teenager, from whom Wendy received her first horse, a small black pony named Napoleon. This darling was Wendy's first love. Little did they realize that their lives would come full-circle, years later, with Gina doing the illustrations for Wendy's poems culminating in this lovely book.

These two talented women, living in the wonderful world of horses, share a love for nature and the western way of life. Their talents express the same kind of life we enjoy - not always an easy one; winters can be extreme, and making a living from the land cannot be taken for granted.

We will always remember the time we attended the 50th Anniversary of the historic Dartigue Lodge on the edge of the timberline near Bottrel. Wendy's mother,

Tillie, was speaking at the dedication. She marvelled at the precision logwork and the meticulous construction of the saddlenotch corners of the Lodge, built in 1934, comparing it to the log dwelling that she had once lived in as a child, saying: "... we might as well have put a roof over our corral and lived in it, because it would have been warmer...!"

Judging from this and other stories we've heard tell, we think Wendy and brother Doug, also an acclaimed cowboy poet, come by their ability with words quite honestly. Sometimes, to keep them interested in their lessons, Tillie, schoolteacher and mom, would ask them to compose anagrams using all of the letters in their names, which might well have been the start of it all.

Over the years, many a friend and neighbour have been royally entertained by Wendy's heartfelt wit delivered along with her friendly smile. She has recited at many Gatherings where Cowboy Poetry is the norm - including the big one at Pincher Creek, Alberta.

It's really special when talents like Wendy's writing and Gina's sketching, unite the realities of the country way of life. It's plain to see they both love life and life loves them. We are delightfully enthralled and entertained by this book of poems and sketches, and you will be too.

Don and Dorothy Edge
Bar 50 Ranch
Cochrane, Alberta

Acknowledgments

I would like to thank all those who are a part of the poems in this book. Their personal stories, characters and lives provided the inspiration for nearly every poem.

Gina's artwork brings each poem to life. It was the author's dream come true to have her illustrate these poems. Thank you, Gina, for this honour.

Thank you to everyone who helped in any way to see this publication through to its end: especially, Terri Belcourt, who typed the poems and scanned and sized the artwork; Daran Fletcher for the cover layout and his invaluable technical input; son-in-law Corey Telfer, for his editing and proofing; long time friends and neighbours Dorothy and Don Edge, for the Foreword; friend and fellow poet Doris Daley, for her kind back-page comments and editing suggestions; and the staff at Friesens Corporation for their advice in preparing the manuscript.

A first book, as a first in any other endeavour, is a challenge and a learning curve. But, it's been fun!

Finally, thank you to my fans, supporters and fellow poets and pickers. Your encouragement has been like a spur in the ribs!

Introduction

Originally, I had intended to write a book of prose on our life as ranch-raised kids in the hills of the Ghost River, west of Cochrane, Alberta. We never went to school, it was done by correspondence. We rode horses, chased cows, and wild horses as part of our every day lives. We read by coal oil lamps and packed water from the well. There were no telephones and no power, so no T.V. 4-H was our social life, and the rest of the time we created our own fun. We had a great time!

I had 20 chapter titles written down. All were based on events that took place in or originated from our log and rail corrals. Then in 1988 Cowboy Poetry arrived with the first Cowboy Poetry Gathering in Canada at Pincher Creek, Alberta. I started writing each chapter title as a poem. However, I got sidetracked with wonderful incidents along the way. Only six of my original chapter titles are in this book.

When you read "A Bronc and a Tire" you will recognize the origin of the book title, "The Corral Bars Are Down". The Bone Pile, The Old Cowhide, The Diamond and a Half Mare, Uncle Audley - A Vanishing Breed and The Invisible Rider are the others. These poems are from the heart. In retrospect they now represent the heritage of a past era. I hope you enjoy them along with the more current poems.

The Land and the Legends

ORIGINAL COWBOY

Once upon a horse
    There was a man
Who, from on his lofty perch
    Did scan
The vast and empty prairie waste
    As he sought, to rid
The permanent taste of
    Stale tobacco from his
Dirty mouth. Oh,
    That cowboy was uncouth.
But then, his eyes were clear,
    His thoughts not a muddled
Chain of emptiness, as he approached
    An unsuspecting steer.
One might wonder at the
    Reason for it all,
And answer, that, everyone
    Has his special call.

BIG HILL COUNTRY

Written in 1972 for, but never submitted to, the Cochrane Big Hill Country history book.

One Hundred years ago I gazed
Upon this Valley where the Buffalo grazed
And the clear swift waters of the Bow River Raced.

My eyes scanned the miles of mountains and hills
My ears heard the melody of the meadow lark's trills
My nose was enchanted with the sweet prairie smells.

I saw no one as I gazed all around,
Only the wild prairie land and the free wild sounds
And an Indian grave – a stone-marked mound.

I came to view often as the years rolled by
From this great rolling hill on the Valley's east side
And watched as settlers came to make homes and
take pride.

And then names took their place and everyone knew
Of Cochrane, Horse Creek, and Dog Pound for a few,
And Jumping Pound, Grande Valley and Morley too.

Then stealthily but swiftly the Valley's face changed
For cattle migrated onto the Buffalo's range,
And the ruts of the travois for steel rails were
exchanged.

Next I saw homes scattered here, nestled there
At the foot of my big hill a town did appear
With a road leading down like a thin winding stair.

The changes came swiftly as the seasons sped past
Coal was discovered but the mines didn't last,
And the wealth of the Valley was found in her gas.

I've been away so long now from the view of my
throne
But today I've come back to gaze all around
And at the fingers of progress I can only astound.

I looked across the Valley to where the great Rockies
spread
And quickly awed again at the old Devil's Head
Then my eyes slipped slowly down the Bow River's
thread.

They flitted on the hills and the Valley before me
And though the Valley was dressed in her modern
array
The wind still brought the scent of that first wild
prairie.

As I stood there and gazed at this land I loved so
I saw the crocus still blooming and heard the larks
trilling low
And I noticed beside me that others stood too.

Then as swiftly as the Westerly Breezes will change
I knew that the Valley was no longer just my great
range
For to others as well now its beauty wasn't strange.

They too felt the breezes as the West Wind blew
Their eyes too were dimmed with a misty-like dew
For this Valley was now home to all of them too.

HEADLINE – "CANADA RETURNED TO THE RED MAN"

A tongue-in-check poem - inspired while travelling up Highway 22 from Cochrane to Drayton Valley. Not all Buffalo are on the plains!

We took the Red Man's land,
Right or wrong as it may be;
We killed off all the buffalo,
With no food – a man's not free.

And so the struggle's been
For a century and more,
And now the Red Man's voice
Says he wants to settle up the score.

We white men are sympathetic
Oh, we won't show prejudice
We'll keep our harmony with the Tribes
We'll give him land and keep the peace;

So while he negotiates for land
Only the Red Man sees that we,
Are raising great herds of buffalo
To fill his fields – he'll soon be free!

GHOST RIVER LEGEND

Written from the Ghost's point of view, this Chief lost his battle with a foe over an Indian maiden.

Ghost River you swift running river
With your blue mountain waters racing by,
You beckon to my heart
You keep calling me back to your side.

Ghost River you swift running river
With your hills sloping down to your cry,
They keep calling me back
To ride among the pines
To hear the west wind breathing its sigh.

Ghost River you swift running river
Your name is the legend of my death,
For many moons have passed
Since I fought with my foe
And now my ghost's a legend to those left.

Ghost River you swift running river
Your rocky bed is my horse's path,
And when the moon is rising full
You will see my shadow ride
And hear the hoof beats pounding as I pass.

Ghost River you swift running river
I will never, never leave your rushing side,
For though my life is over
Still in death I live,
When the moon is full my ghost will always ride.

THE BUFFALO SKULL

We were kids playing Cowboys and Indians
Down in the brush by the bog
When I noticed something sticking up in the muck
Right by an old mossy log.

It was sticking up through the mud
Right near the boggy cow trail
Which would near stick a horse that crossed it
For he'd sink clear down to his tail.

We saw it was the tip of a horn
At first we thought it a cow,
But when we dug in and around
It didn't seem to be that somehow.

We found it was a great massive skull
And getting it out was right tough,
But when done we were excited to see
The gigantic skull of a buff.

Preserved in the mud for how long?
It could have been hundreds of years,
A find that any Westerner'd proudly hang on his wall
In place of the Longhorn steer.

LEGEND OF THE MOUNTAIN MAN

The only poem I've written purely from imagination.

The towering Rockies etched darkly on a midnight sky
And the gurgling mountain stream
Glinted in the moonlight
Of my dream.

And there he came...
Riding through the pass in my mind's eye,
The Mountain Man
Now only in a dream he passes by

His horse, not refined
By standards we now tote
But heavy boned, deep girthed,
Sinewy muscled, sure-footed like a mountain goat.

He lights beside the stream to make his camp
Silently unsaddles, then removes the packs;
Hobbles up the pair with buckskin thongs,
Unwraps the meat from greying flour sacks.

Lights his fire with flints pulled from a can
Quickly strips the venison with his knife,
Wipes the blade on his buckskin legging
Encrusted it seems, by a habit practised all his life.

I'm closer now, I see his hair
Long, shaggy, streaking gray
Like the mountain sides
Where dark firs alternate with slides like night
and day.

His coat, a smoky buckskin,
You can smell it in the dampness of the night-
time air.
Past the buckskin leggings, on his feet,
Moccasins, silent footwear, beaded by a red
hand with skill and care.

The meat is ready as he stabs it with a fork
Biting one end, he reaches for his hip,
Takes the hunting knife once more;
Cuts off a chew almost at his lips.

Finished, he puts away his tools,
Ties the meat on a high branch of a tree,
Unwraps his pack, pulls out a fur covered roll
Soon, he's in his dreams like me.

And so, the darkness of the night pulls down her
shade
And the Mountain Man is but a distant legend,
In a dream of another time, it seems,
It's now passed on to you, my friend.

SUNDANCE

Laurie Johnson, a well known rancher in the Cochrane area told me this story the winter I worked for him and his wife, Jean. I was 16 at the time.

We sat sunning ourselves on blocks of wood
In the doorway of the old log barn,
Taking a break from our morning chores
As they were almost done.

I remember the conversation
As if it were yesterday,
Though it's been over forty years
Since the old rancher had his say.

He asked me, "Have you heard of Harry Longabaugh?"
I answered, "I didn't think I did"
"Well," he said, "You must have heard
Of the Outlaw called the Sundance Kid?"

"You mean the guy who rode with Butch Cassidy
During the days of his outlaw fame?"
And then I remembered Harry Longabaugh
Was the Sundance Kid's real name.

The old rancher went on with his story
That I'll tell you here tonight,
And when I'm done you too may wonder
If the movie ended right.

He said, "Harry was my Dad's best man
When he got married in '91.
It took place down High River way
Before the Wildbunch had their fun."

I was thinking of the wedding picture
    I'd seen hanging on his bedroom wall,
I'd not realized that one name beneath
    Was that of the famous outlaw.

Then the rancher rose up from his block,
    And leaned on the frame of the door
And as he looked wistfully out
    He said, "I want to tell you a little more".

"Harry and Butch never died
    In South America like the stories say,
Harry came up here and changed his name
    And lived to a ripe old age".

In confidence he named the community
    Where Harry had lived out his life
Also the pseudonym he took,
    And, I think, he had a family and wife.

At that the conversation ended
    And the old rancher went back to his chores
And we never again spoke about it
    Though years later I wished I knew more.

For you see, lost in the recesses of my mind
    Like an outlaw in the Breaks of Wyoming
Is knowledge worth as much as a good train robbery,
    It's Harry's last pseudonym!

Oh, I had chances to ask the old rancher
    For it's not long since he crossed the great divide,
But each time I backed off for I felt I'd forsake
    A trust I had sealed up inside.

Besides did I really want to know
    And destroy secret thoughts I've kept hid
About whether my friends who live in that place
    Might even be ancestors of the Sundance Kid?

Vicarious Views of the Cattle Business

DOWN ON THE RANCH – 1992

*Written for the Pincher Creek Poetry Gathering Program
- an unfavourable spring for the cowman in
the South - but it got better.*

This year down on the ranch
    Everyone hopes there's the chance
That the price of beef on the hoof
    Will still keep us under the roof.

We wonder if the steers in the pasture
    Will bring in as much as last year?
Or will they drop off too,
    And leave all the bills overdue?

Who knows what will take place
    In the world's economic race,
Can we survive as our fathers before us,
    Or will we be the ones on the bus?

Well, a cowman won't worry about it,
    'Cause the spring calves are all looking fit,
And the old saying still seems to ring true –
    "Hang onto the old cow's tail –
        she'll always pull you through!"

WHAT GOES AROUND COMES AROUND

I think the cycle's tightened - it's already coming around since I wrote this 10 years ago!

A hundred years ago and more
You could really find some size,
For those big old steers are written up
And those old record books don't lie.

I wonder who really started
To change the size of cattle,
And why did ranchers breed them down,
Was there no argument or battle?

Could it be that lack of feed
Was the reason why,
Or did someone think it cute
When some bull threw pint sized?

Well, the cycle is completed
And we're back to lots of size;
Now will the cycle bend again
Until we realize,

That someone thinks he's started
A new fangled cattle craze
'Cause he's got some pint sized cattle
And he's turned them out to graze;

His neighbour's cows are hanging
Right on that fence line
And the bull jumps in and figures
He's really doing fine.

Now in a year or two these two,
It's plain to see,
Have got two herds much smaller
And maybe that's where we should be.

So we buy their pint sized bulls
Thinking we'll get right in there fast
Not realizing we're just fulfilling
A fad that just won't last.

You see as time goes on its almost
Two thousand and eight-five,
And in another ten
The cycle will come alive.

So if you don't like to see
The cattle that now are found
Just hang around a hundred years
Your type will come around.

THE CALVY COW

A woman's point of view.

The calvy cow stands quietly
    And chews her cud so placidly
You check and check and check and check
    Not a danged thing's happened yet.

You're thinkin' to yourself, I'm wrong,
    Why's she hangin' on and on?
Are my eyes deceivin' me?
    Surely she'll calve by Wednesday!

You're already thinkin' in your dome
    That you or the wife will be stayin' home
On this weekend that you'd long planned
    At the cattlemen's conference, I'll be danged!

There's the thought that's saved the day
    The wife won't mind to stay away
She's still got the income tax to do,
    And it'll save gettin' in a sitter too.

Now the scene is slowly shifting,
    The doom from you is quickly lifting
But it's quickly settled down upon,
    The better half in this here poem.

She schemes and prays and herself checks now,
    To hurry up that calvy cow,
But alas, it is to no avail,
    On Friday the cowman drives out the trail.

His wife left standing there alone
Amidst the dishes, kids and ringing phone.
Then she remembers why she's there
That old cow's been left in her trusty care.

She pulls on her boots, her coat, her mitts,
There's one thing sure she'll keep her wits.
She walks briskly out to check on things
May as well see what this day brings.

As all you cow wives out there know
The dust ain't even settled on the road
When you round the corner of the barn and see
The whole herd standing, waiting patiently.

But your eyes are wandering past the bunch
As though they're playing out a hunch
And sure enough, standing so solitarily,
A cow, beneath the old lone tree.

You don't so much as check the rest
It ain't even an intuition test,
You trudge out through the snow and lumps,
Checking to see if her old tail's up.

Not yet, she's just switchin' and switchin'
At least there must be somethin' itchin'.
So back you go and do all the chores
And then Vi drives in to pick up that horse.

You have a coffee and chew the fat,
All the time your mind is off on that
Old calvy cow out there alone,
Is she still standing or is she prone?

Finally the trailer goes out the lane,
And you dash out to check again.
This time, sure enough she's moved,
Her tail is up her sides are heaved.

She's turning herself around and around
Then she's flat out on the ground.
You sneak up behind to have a look,
Just as you thought, the water bag's broke.

Well, you figure she's doing fine
She's big and old, give her a bit of time.
So back to the house you quietly sneak,
You'll give her an hour then take a peek.

The dishes all washed, the vacuuming done,
Time to check and see the fun
That old girl should be calved by now,
She's a great big old and framey cow.

But the hand of fear is gripping at your heart
For she's an unknown from the Olds Auction Mart.
No telling what her habits were before
So out you go to check once more.

And soon your diagnostic glance
Tells you nothing has advanced,
She's just the same as when last you looked
It's time for action – before your record's cooked.

You don't panic but there is alarm
As you slowly haze her up into the barn
Then back to the house and phone the neighbour
"Can you come give me a hand with this cow in
labour?"

While you're waiting for the neighbour to come
    You get the puller, chains and come-a-long.
When he drives in, you're all set for the pull
    Still acting nonchalant and cool.

He throws on the rope – she doesn't choke
    At least the old girl's halter broke!
Well things check out to be coming straight
    But we'd best not any longer wait.

So Bill goes to work and puts on the chains
    And the old girl shows she's got some pains
We hook on the puller and bring it on
    Boy, that calf was big and long.

Well, he turns out to be a fine big bruiser
    And I'm quite pleased we're not a loser
Then we go in and get cleaned up,
    And on a cup of coffee sup.

The next day, the boss arrives back home
    Asks what's happened while he's been gone,
"Oh", I said, "We've got a new calf,
    Not much else other than that."

This of course is what he said
    When I told him we'd pulled or it'd be dead,
You likely didn't leave her work enough,
    I said, "At 120 pounds – her job was tough."

THE OLD COWHIDE

At the price of cowhides (at this time of Mad Cow),
maybe we should cut costs and get them back out.

A rusty hook on the outside wall
Right behind the old barn door
Brings memories of an old cowhide
Which hung there years before.

The old cowhide was used so much
That we wore out three or four,
But it didn't matter for they were cheap
Though they did a lot of chores.

For every morning I'd let down the hide
And drag it out into place,
Then Dad would load it up
As he cleaned out each stall space.

He'd saddle Old Congo who pranced and danced
While he dallied the rope 'round the horn
And take off dragging that loaded cowhide
Then dump it below the hill by the barn.

In the winter time us kids would run
Down to the bottom of that hill,
Then jump on the hairy side up
And ride back to the barn for a thrill.

Now that old hide was also used
To drag in cold calves in the spring,
It also hauled rocks and helped many a horse
To overcome his fear of anything.

So you can see an old cowhide
Can be a hand for many a chore,
But the thing that I wonder about
Is why they aren't used any more?

For:

Today's rancher buys a big fancy spreader
Then he needs a tractor to pull it,
Now he buys a Bobcat to clean down the aisle
And joins an exercise club to keep fit.

On top of all that he pays a horse trainer
To teach some common sense to his horse
And he's bought a rock picker,
And a 4-wheel drive – to haul cold calves in of course.

Now a $30 cowhide could do just as well
And who cares what the banker would say,
'Cause the loan's all paid with money left over
To go on a nice holiday.

A TALE OF TWO STEERS

Truth is always better than fiction.

The couple drove in our yard
    One warm midsummer day,
Friends and neighbours of the folks
    Is what I'm wont to say.

They came in and were seated
    On the sofa near the door
(Our log house was very small
    Being one main room, one floor).

Now Mother was putting on the coffee,
    While Dad checked the fire in the stove
When the lady turned to him and asked,
    "The reason here we drove,

Is we wondered if you had seen
    My two steers which seem lost,
They're three year olds and are quite fat,
    And I'd like to ship them very fast.

But we've ridden everywhere,
    And not a hair we've seen
Of these two big steers of mine
    Maybe you know where they've been?"

My Dad was looking in the stove
    When she had queried thus,
He put the lid down gently and
    Said, "Yes, I saw them just

Last week in Calgary
    At the stockyards right where
Your husband was unloading them –
    I'm sure they were the pair".

There was silence for a moment
    Then she turned to her man and asked,
"Is what Jim said the truth?"
    He said, "Yes, dear, it's a fact".

The big steers were never mentioned
    As we talked of neighbours, cows and fence
But when they left we wondered,
    If their drive home was tense!

CALGARY
STOCKYARDS
BURP
OX

COW CHIPS

This one's closer to reality every day.

When we speak of cow chips
I'm sure you'd watch your step
If you walked behind the cows
In the field where they are kept.

Well, now there's another cow chip
Where you don't need to watch your stand,
It's that little micro chip
That will replace your antique brand.

It's the modern cowboy way
To plant a chip beneath the hide
Maybe have a printout on the saddle horn
When around the herd he rides,

That tells which cow he's watching,
When she met with Old Man Bull,
If her calf sucked at 5 A.M.,
And yes, her stomach's full!

Now I've pondered other uses
For this new exotic chip,
Could the odd wife be tempted
To implant it on the loin above his hip?

Some night when he stumbles home
Not quite sure who gave the ride,
The wife could easy gun that chip
While he lies snoring on his side.

She then installs the read-out
    On the headboard of the bed
Right behind her pillow,
    Where it's hid but easily read.

Now the next time he's out late
    She yawns and falls asleep,
He's just socializing with his cronies
    And the bull chips are knee-deep!

THE RESURRECTED COW

You've seen the pointed finger
Aimed at the cowman who took a chance
On buying shares in some stock
That left empty pockets in his pants.

On seeing such derision
Making the loser out a fool
I'll ask a pointed question
My tone of voice, a little cool –

"Have you ever bought a cow
With a sleek and shiny hide
Took her home and turned her out,
To find the next day that she'd died?"

"Yes," the finger pointer answers,
"It's happened once or twice,
The seller said she was sound as a dollar
Guess I got some bad advice."

"So," I said, "at least the guy
With the worthless paper in his hand,
Can trunk it for his grandkids
Hoping they will understand,

The note he's stapled to it
Which will read like this somehow,
'If these shares check out as valued
You've got a resurrected cow' ".

EGG CRATE

THE DECISION

Let's keep her one more year
    She looks real good this fall,
Oh, she's old alright, but
    One more calf she'll call.

In fact, she's looking better
    Than I've ever seen her look,
She'll be fine for another year
    And he closed his tally book.

Her heifer was the best
    In the weaning pen today;
I'll feed her a few more pellets
    I know she'll be okay.

Of course, if I sold her now
    She'd weigh her very best,
But we might get one more heifer
    To put out with the rest.

A few days later when he went out
    To do the morning chores
He looked out in the pasture field
    And was pierced right to the core.

For the old girl lay plumb lifeless
    Right where her body'd dropped
And the only conclusion reached was
    That her poor old heart had stopped.

And so one economical decision
    Made over coffee and a piece of toast,
Is now just a skull and horns
    Hanging on a gray fence post.

GRAND
CHAMPION
BQ

THE TWENTY-FIVE YEAR CLUB

Presented to the Twenty-Five Year Hereford Club BBQ at Bert Powlesland's, July 29, 1990.

There are lots of yarns to spin
And lots of hands to shake
When you've been in Herefords 25 years
It's nice to take a break.

It's nice to gather once a year
And have a little fun
Even tell some stories close to truth
'Cause newcomers aren't around.

Like, you've pulled a Hereford calf or two
Or sewed up the odd prolapse
Even stuck a needle in that front tit
That's near dragging on the grass.

Yes, you might even mention
The time you bought that pricey bull
The one which sired those real great calves,
The kind most ranchers cull.

But then we know the talk will shift
To how the Hereford cow will yield
A decent calf most every year
Without two tons of feed.

And how she's usually gentle
And doesn't need a 6 foot wire
To keep her home – the exotic that jumps in,
He's the one that needs it higher.

You'll reminisce about the shows
    And of course the Big Bull Sale,
After 25 years of these events
    Each has his favourite tales.

You might discuss the doubts you've had,
    Like should you cross with white or black,
Or maybe use something that's all red,
    Or has a big stripe down it's back.

But when you eat a Hereford steak
    Your mind is put to rest
Your confidence is right back up,
    'Cause you know you raise the best.

A WOMAN'S POINT OF VIEW ON WORKING CATTLE AND OTHER FARM CHORES

There's a strange thing happens to a man
When he starts to sort or work his cattle,
It seems he loses all common sense
And he's prone to yell or battle.

Now the wife and kids are usual targets
For this verbal abusive prattle,
Even Morrie Goetjen says when the thunder roars,
He knows his Dad's up there sorting cattle.

And I remember one branding day
When Mum and Dad came to help
This calf escaped and my loving man
Gave a curse and a yelp,

As the calf streaked off across the field
With Walter in full chase,
I knew the words flowing from his lips
Would bring him full disgrace.

I knew my mother had never heard
Such words in all her ranching life,
And wondered what she was thinking
Of this man who'd made me his wife.

But my mother was doubled over laughing,
And I heard her weakly exclaim,
"Whether young or old I can't believe
How they're all the same!"

One night we went for coffee
At the home of some of our friends,
Some husband/wife stories revealed
The humour never ends.

Like the guy who knocked his wife on the head
With the bucket on his loader,
She went to Didsbury for some stitches
And grew a little older.

Not long after, once again
Her head got in the way,
When the bar on the cow stanchion
Fell down – more stitches on that day.

Then they were throwing firewood
Into an old granary to keep it dry
When a block fell down from the top window
Almost making her cry.

Once again her head took the blow
And her husband kindly said
If it had hit her anywhere else
I'm sure she would be dead.

Well he urged her to go up to the hospital
She said, "Dear you're down a litre,
I'll not go there again for stitches,
They'll report you as a wife beater".

Gina ©

THOSE BEAUTIFUL HEIFERS

Why is it that the beauty
    Of the heifer that draws your eye
Rarely perpetrates itself
    In the offspring by her side?

I guess she's a little like the woman
    Groomed and dressed right to a "T",
Lots of eye appeal its true
    But not much substance underneath.

That heifer came in dry this year
    Last year she lost her calf,
Guess it's time to toughen up
    And send her down the garden path.

Kind of like our fancy woman
    Who you find can't cook or clean,
But your friends think you have a winner
    'Cause they've judged only what they've seen.

Oh, that heifer looks good in the herd,
    Cars slow down to have a look
Well next time they want to see her,
    She'll be hanging on the hook.

Not quite so simple with our woman
    For that decision there's no reverse,
We must live with what we've chosen,
    And trust our judgments don't grow worse.

Mostly Horses

ALWAYS BET ON #8

I never let Uncle Bill forget this one.

It was a family tradition
That on the 24th of May
Some of us would get together
And head to Calgary for the day.

And with a few bucks in our pockets
We'd have a little fun,
Our destination, Victoria Park,
To watch the ponies run.

Well this one year Uncle Bill came
And he was giving me some tips
On how to pick a horse so I'd be sure
To cash in on some chips.

His advice was to always bet on No. 8,
(And maybe sometimes Four),
And so we perused the program
To see if we could score.

Well, in the first race sure enough
Was a mare called Boutique Belle
A sorry looking racehorse, I thought,
But who was I to tell,

For she was packing No. 8
And Uncle Bill swore by his formula of course;
Although I contested quite strongly
That maybe we should reconsider – this horse.

She was long and sway backed
And her head could have filled a bag,
And I was more than a little concerned
That my two bucks would be lost on this nag.

When my eye glanced at the board
    She was the longshot of the field,
And as we headed for the wickets
    My nerve would almost yield,

But, I gritted my teeth and bet her,
    Then raced out to the fence
To see if old Boutique Belle
    Could disprove common sense!

Well, I could hardly contain myself
    As they swung the turn for home,
Boutique Belle was coming fast
    And in first place she sure did come.

I delightedly went to cash my win
    When the win board said "thirty-two",
And looked around for Uncle Bill
    To see if he was cashing in too,

But when I finally spotted him
    He was tearing up his ticket,
And I asked, "what are you doing that for,
    Aren't you heading for the wicket?"

He said, "No, are you?" and he had
    A sheepish look;
I said, "You didn't bet on No. 8?"
    He said, "No, it 's Four I took".

And so the lesson I learned from Uncle Bill that day
    Is that when you're prone to give advice,
Be sure to bet on No. 8 yourself
    Or you may have to pay the price!

EQUINE FASHION

At the Medicine Hat indoor rodeo in the 1990's.

Last night I went to a rodeo
    I hadn't been to one for awhile
The horses all looked shaggy
    But I was told "It's the latest style".

The manes were long and flowing
    In all the timed events;
I could see that at roaching manes
    Not much time'd been spent.

It was pointed out to me
    By a person in "the know",
That long and flowing tails
    Were also all the "go"!

And that fetlocks haired and woolly
    Were a coveted asset
Why, it'll take 30 years to breed hair
    Back on smooth fetlocks, I'll bet.

And then I got to thinking
    About the horses at our place,
Hardly touched by human hand
    They never took up arena space;

With flowing manes and unpulled tails
    And fetlocks in a shaggy state,
I think I'll start showing them
    'Cause they're arena Fashion Plates!

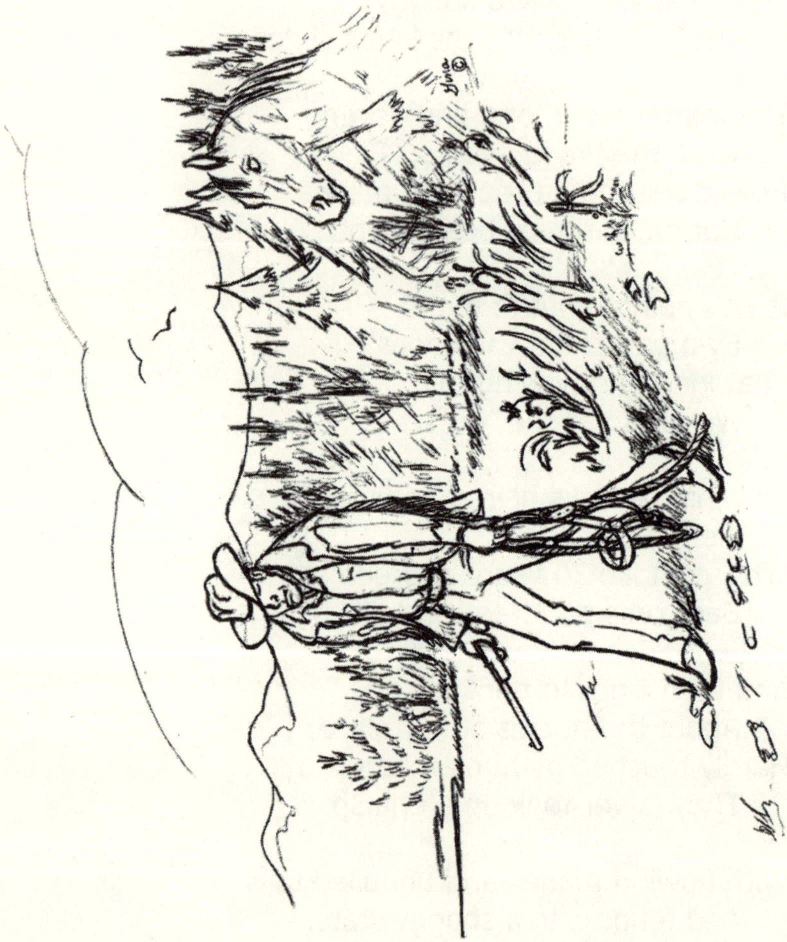

THE BONE PILE

The second cowboy poem I wrote. I was afraid to recite it, but did it at Pincher Creek in 1988. I knew it hit a chord when I saw tears in the eyes of old ranchers sitting in the audience. It was later filmed as a CBC news documentary.

Now you all know no rancher's lived
    That ain't had some livestock die
A calvin' cow, a calf not right,
    Or Ol' Faithful – that no meathorse man could buy.

Have you ever asked, or stopped to wonder
    What kind of graveyard receives this lot?
Let shivers run up your curvatured spine
    While I describe where the animal bones rot.

Now some ranchers let them lie
    Right where their bodies drop,
And others drag them out to the coulee
    Or on the other side of the crop.

The more modern environmental livestock man
    Picks up his telephone,
He calls out the man with the dirty gray van
    To pick up the meat and bones.

But out at our place when I was a kid
    We had a regular place for dead critters
We always called it the "Bone Pile",
    It was a place that could give you the jitters.

For scattered beneath the jack pines
    In a small open hollow past the lake
Are the bones of horses and cattle,
    (Dogs were buried in graves – marked by a willow
                                        stake).

I've wondered if there's a book upstairs
Giving names from the four-legged file,
Let's say that there is and flip through the pages
Listing the names from our old Bone Pile.

Of the cows lying out in that cemetery
I'll recall here just a few
For time erases names and events,
Though their bones still lie 'neath the dew.

There's Pansy, a calf from an old milk cow
That died giving birth at two
And my own first cow, Old Bobtail,
We couldn't cure her dysentery flu.

There's a number of calves not born in time,
A steer that fell through the ice,
A cow or two – cast with their backs down a hill;
I know none of this sounds nice.

I remember Old Bumpy who died of bloodworms
(Of horses I recall quite a few)
And Napoleon my very first kid's pony
Who fell through the ice on the slough.

Then there are a bunch of "no names"
Whose demise was granted by lead
For the meat from their bones fed the mink that were skinned
To make hats for elite ladies' heads.

Also, out there Pint, my old Pinto lies,
A victim of equine sleeping sickness;
Just a little horse all personality and heart
And the years have not let me think less.

But the last one I remember was the saddest
    When the 30-30 came down off the wall,
"It was the hardest thing that I've ever done"
    I later heard my Dad recall.

Old Congo had been his saddle horse
    For more than twenty-five years,
He'd been faithful and true and worked hard all his life
    It brought the rest of the family to tears,

When Old Congo lay dying in the dust by the barn
    A victim of old age and time
As we heard the shot echo out – each had his own thoughts
    Knowing Dad was just being kind.

Then as we heard Dad's old truck going out
    And around the lake's north side
My thoughts were on the Old Bone Pile
    The destination of Congo's last ride.

Memories of those many friends that are gone
    Flashed through my mind once again
Memories of the yipping of coyotes and low moan of bears
    Paying their respects still remain.

So now you've heard this graveyard's story
    I'll try to leave you with a bit of a smile,
For I can still hear my mother saying,
    "When I'm gone – just drag me out to the bone pile."

THE DIAMOND AND A HALF MARE

Dad had run some wild horses in
Off the hills of the Old Bar C,
And among the lot was an old black mare
Well aged it was plain to see.

Her wither was sharp and high
And her muzzle was silvery gray,
And her back dipping low
Showed well her years in its sway.

Her mane was long and tangled,
Her tail near drug the ground,
Her ribs and hip bones were protruding;
She'd wintered hard when found.

Her left hip was well marked
With the Diamond and a Half Brand,
An iron not used in twenty years
By either the owner or his hands.

Her back and rump were mottled
With the gray of sucking ticks,
And her hooves were broke and ragged
Where the rocks had got their licks.

But her eyes so keen and sharp
Watched our every move,
And her ears flicked back and forth
While the young stuff milled a groove.

We cut away the young slicks
Then ran her in the chute,
Dad pulled her mane and tail, while Doug and I
Snapped ticks on the gate planks with our boots.

She never fought the chute,
Just stood while we picked off ticks,
Though her nostrils would flare and she'd snort
If we moved a little too quick.

We turned her back in the corral
Leaving her there for the day,
In the morning when the three of us rode out
The old mare led the way;

She passed us on the trail
As we rode to the river and hills,
Waited for us at the North gate
While Dad opened it, she stood, impatiently still,

Then trotted through and led on
Up the range to the river bank,
And down the short cut trail's steep incline
Then sniffed the running water, but never drank.

We sat and watched as she crossed the Ghost
On the way to her hills – she was free,
She never paused or looked back as she trotted
Up the draw, and disappeared in the trees.

Well, we never saw her again,
But while riding the river the next spring
I saw the bald eagles circling high in the hills
And these thoughts in my mind took wing;

Were they circling some carrion they'd found,
Could it be the old mare had cashed in?
And did her spirit now soar as free as an eagle
On the warm, spring chinook wind?

A BRONC AND A TIRE

The "man" in this one was my Dad, Jim Richards.

That big brown horse was wild
    There in the old round pen
When the rope snaked out and settled
    Around his neck and mane.

He was big and muscled
    With Percheron showing strong
His age was all of nine or ten
    And he'd not had a halter on.

You can picture all the fire
    Exploding 'neath his silky hide
As the rope was quickly wrapped
    Around the snubbing tree and tied.

He pulled back hard and cut his wind
    As the loop tightened 'round his throat;
The man took his breaking halter
    And quickly moved up on the rope.

Sliding it over the bronc's nose and ears
    He quietly snapped the latch,
The bronc's sides heaved his breath was strained,
    As he gave him a little scratch,

Then stepped back and wrapped the shank
    Around the snubbing tree,
Loosened off the lariat,
    That bronc thought he was free.

He stood there for a moment
    As he caught a bit of wind
Then lunged away, but that halter
    Soon turned him in a spin.

I could smell the dusty bark
When his shoulder scraped the logs
And you could hear how mad he was
'Cause he squealed just like a hog.

He fought there for awhile
But soon he knew the score,
Just step up on that shank a bit
And the halter pulled no more.

He was left tied up there for the night
Then in the early morn,
The man led him down to water
Snubbed to the saddle horn.

I think it was a day or two
He was tended to like this
Fed a little hay,
And led to water once or twice.

And though the man worked him
And sacked him all around,
It was plain to see
He wasn't going to settle down.

So he decided to put an end
To this old bronc's snort
By tying a tire to the shank-
Not too long and not too short.

Once loose he didn't circle
Within the round corral
But headed for the bars
And smashed them all to hell.

BOINK
BOINK
HELP
YIKES

Then he hit the big corral
    And really went into high,
Did a circle and headed, for
    The wire gate and open sky.

As that tire hit the ground
    With each stride he took,
It was plain to see the wire gate
    Would be slightly more than shook.

He hit it with such force
    I can still hear the snap of posts,
And wire breaking as it stretched
    As if going coast to coast.

That horse turned on speed
    No one ever knew he had,
Tore down the hill, through the brush
    And out the other side.

Finally, he stopped on the open hill
    After fifteen minutes or so,
And the man walked up beside him
    And said a gentle "Whoa".

He never moved a muscle,
    Just moved his ears a bit,
But he'd worked up quite a lather
    Before he'd finally quit.

When the man untied the rope
    That horse stepped up to him,
And with one eye cocked upon the tire
    He sidled past its rim.

He led back to the barn
    Like it was the norm,
But the words uttered by the man
    Could have raised a storm!

For pieces of the gate were scattered
    For a hundred yards and some,
And that's when the Gallus* gate got built
    In between the barns back home.

*Gallus Gate - wooden swinging gate with high posts on either side and pole across the top. Named after its inventor.

UNCLE AUDLEY – A VANISHING BREED

Audley Richards, my Dad's brother, epitomized the old time cowboy.

He was tall and slim
    With a twinkle in his eye,
His Stetson hat was grey
    The kind with the crown real high.

He always rode a horse
    That a cowboy would call good,
Meaning he could do some work
    And take you down the road.

Uncle Audley was a horseman,
    A little hard, some would say,
But you knew a horse he rode
    Could pack you night and day.

His left arm had been injured
    And had healed up at an angle,
But this was no deterrent
    When it came time for him to wrangle.

One day I saw him bring in
    A wild bunch all alone,
Corralled them at our place
    Then cut out the stud – a big bald-faced blue roan.

He took the rope down off his saddle
    And with the coils on his left arm
He front-footed that big stud
    And brought him to the ground.

His moves were smooth and quiet
    And as he tied that big horse up
He saw me watching through the logs,
    And asked me to get some table salt in Mother's
        metal cup.

He was waiting when I returned,
    I passed it to his bloodstained hand
And watched him fill the empty pockets,
    The horse – no longer king of his wild band.

I think of this day whenever
    I see horsemen without skills,
Who call out vets in white coats
    With tranquillizer guns and pills.

Yes, Uncle Audley,
    It leaves me sad to think
That you were one of a special breed,
    That's now almost extinct.

Gina
©

Rodeos and Cowboys

A SALUTE TO NORTHLANDS CFR & FARMFAIR

Tom Bews was one of Canada's finest Bronc Riders in the 1970's and 1980's.
The art for the section page is also for this poem.

The red man dipped his silent paddle
 In waters leading to the Fort,
To trade his furs for shiny trinkets
 Is what our history books report.

They tell us how the settlers came
 When furs became so very scarce,
And how the Missionary and Red Coat
 Were the ones who tamed the Canadian West;

And how the fort became a city
 And was the hub of our North Land,
How grain fields covered travois tracks
 And oil rigs took their noisy stand.

All these things and many more
 Made this crossroads to the North
When twenty years ago – a dream
 Of the big Fair and Rodeo sprang forth.

Edmonton would now be home
 For Farmfair – with major cattle shows,
And for our Canadian Pro Cowboys,
 To hold their Finals Rodeos.

At that first historic show
 We walked the cattle barns and lanes,
And saw all those new breeds showing
 Who now boast they're household names.

The first rodeo was home to us
    As we came down from Dawson Creek
Where we'd moved to from the south,
    And family and friends we saw all week.

And so it's been for twenty years,
    Yes, we've missed some it's true,
But in 1991 we were there,
    And those old friends were all renewed.

The cattle shows were very fine
    And the Quarter Horse sale was great,
But it's the rodeo that inspired me
    With this story I'll relate.

Of an old bronc rider and his wife
    Who sat in seats two rows below,
He'd ridden these finals here himself,
    Now, nearly twenty years ago.

Tonight he came to sit and watch
    That old bronc now past his prime
For his son would ride him out
    As he bucked for his last time.

The man had ridden this old horse
    To pay windows of bygone days
But now his son would ride him out
    As young fans cheered, I watched the play.

You see no one but I knew who he was
    In that section where we sat,
They all watched the kid ride out
    And missed the real drama in this act.

I wondered how fame could be so fickle
    How could this legend of the past
Be surrounded by those who watched,
    Yet they saw only half the cast?

The couple sat as the announcer built
    The drama of this bronc's last ride
And I wondered at the other story
    When their eyes met, and they both smiled.

Then the gate swung open wide
    For me horse and rider were a blur,
While I watched the old bronc rider
    As in his mind each jump he spurred.

The ride was over at the whistle
    And the crowd cheered my hero's son,
But I sat silent as I wondered,
    Where nearly twenty years had gone.

But thoughts pass on in a fleeting moment
    When you're tapped by an old friend
And you realize once more,
    The spirit here will never end.

Yes, Northlands is the modern Fort
    A Crossroads as people come from everywhere,
Heck, this year you might get lucky,
    And meet a cowboy poet there!

THE TROPHY

Frankie Cockx and Walter Vaughan

Two men stepped upon a train
    At Northlands Edmonton
Heading to respective rooms
    At the Finals in '91.

They both wore Stetsons
    And had on good boots and jeans,
One sported greying hair,
    And neither one was lean.

Each nodded to the other
    And there was silence for a bit
Then one asked – "That bronze
    Are you still holding it?"

"Yes", the gray haired one replied,
    "It's still upon my mantle,
A treasure I won't part with
    Though I might lose my land and cattle."

"I really should come out and dust it off,
    To make sure that it's still there,
'Cause it should have been mine,
    If the judges had been fair."

Both of them had a chuckle,
    Then the winner pulled back his fold
"At 50 my kids gave me this buckle,
    They weren't given in those days we rode."

They chatted and reminisced
    'Til the train stopped downtown,
Catching up on all the years
    They'd not seen each other around.

You see, it was way back in '56
    That they were just two country boys
Riding steers at Calgary
    So their spurs could make a noise.

Frankie had his trophy
    With only one point more
Than Walt who finished second
    Because there'd been a recount on the score.

KILGORE & THE BRONC RIDER

When he first started riding in the F.C.A., Doug drew Kilgore (one of Joe Bardgett's rankest bucking horses) at a lot of the rodeos. To sum it up, the pick-up men were not kept busy!

There was a red hoss called Kilgore
That Doug wanted to draw just once more
But what was the use
To draw that cayuse
When it cost money to launder his drawers!

THE STEER DECKER

Roy Groves was a good hand in both the F.C.A. and Pro circuits.

There was a steer decker named Roy
  Decking steers was his chief pride and joy,
    But an itty bitty beer
    Gave him the first double steer
That's been known to any decking cowboy.

THE BULL RIDER

A bull rider from Cochrane.

A bragging bull rider named Bill
Drew Tiger to give him a thrill
But that wily old bull
Filled Bill's mouth plumb full
Of dirt, when he lit in a mole hill!

THE CLOWN

Besides being a top hand in four events, Dave MacDonald was well known for his bullfighting in the F.C.A. This incident took place at the Innisfail Rodeo, in the mid-1960's. Later, Dave went on to win the Canadian Steer Wrestling Championship .

There once was a clown called Dave
About whom everyone raved
But at one rodeo
His undies did show
When a bull hooked his pants and they gave!

THE BALLAD OF THE COWBOY'S BRONC

The first cowboy poem I wrote - back in the early 60's when Doug and his friend, Dave Argent, were first riding broncs. They always had excuses as to what happened. While they were telling me their tales of woe after arriving home from a rodeo - I wrote this. (Sounded a lot more romantic to me than "my shank was too short (or too long)", etc., etc.)!

They put his wild horse in the chute,
He screwed his saddle down,
Then climbed upon the quivering beast,
The fight was really on.

The gate was opened wide you see
And horse and man were out
The wondering crowd did watch the fight,
Which one would win the bout?

The man did rake the horse with spurs
From mane to flank and more,
The horse did pound the dusty ground
With hooves both hind and fore.

The crowd was yelling on its feet
The rider "he will win",
Then that fool did wave his hat,
The girl, she caught his grin.

The horse, he sensed this show-off act
He bucked so straight and high
The cowboy lost his solid grip
And sailed out through the sky.

He came to earth with sounding thud,
  The bronc had won the round,
The man lay in a crumpled heap
  Upon that dusty ground.

And this to you my bronco friends
  Is but a warning heed,
Quit looking for that little gal,
  And watch your bucking steed.

SALUTE TO CLIFF WILLIAMSON

In 1988 Cliff was so close to winning the world,
and had not yet won the $50,000 at Calgary.

Just this afternoon we heard
"There's a roast for Cliff tonight"
Too bad, I thought, it's a bit too late
To whip off a poem that's right.

But then as I was mopping the floor
A little voice came in my head,
"It's never too late to write a poem
For a neighbour or a friend."

"But there's no time," I argued,
"To gather facts from far and near,"
"So what," that voice spoke up again,
"You have known Cliff for years."

Then past thoughts started coming
And I've set them down right here,
Though it is a shortened version
Of Cliff's calf roping career.

The first time I remember Cliff
Was in Cochrane at a Little Britches show,
Though just a kid on an old cream horse
His loop looked like a Pro's.

And I heard people comment then
That if he kept that up
He'd win the "world" some day,
And drink from the Winner's Cup.

Yes, Cliff, we saw you win
    For years in all those little shows,
Like Dog Pound in the F.C.A.
    And then finally in the Pro's.

Your name became a household word
    Among ropers everywhere
And even bronc and bull riders
    Almost came to care.

At Calgary for years it seems,
    We've cheered you on for gold,
But every time that pot gets close
    You've put our cheers on hold.

The same holds true at CFR
    The calves are big and tough,
Or the barrier snaps the red flag up,
    Or a loop's not tight enough.

But then we all knew the NFR
    In '88 would be
The place Cliff would make cheers ring loud
    In the True North strong and free.

So now we sit out the winter
    Making our next year's bets,
On the famous Kids from Westbrook School
    And just how far they'll get.

Or better still let's lay our green
    On whose dream will first unfurl,
Will George Fox be called to Nashville,
    Or Cliff just win the "World"?

CHUCKWAGON DRIVER

Dedicated to the memory of my Uncle, Ed Larsen, who drove a chuckwagon at Calgary back in the late 1950's.

It's spring, the grass is green
    Horses look good as they're brought in.
Soft, but fresh, their hooves need a trim
    Before they're harnessed once again.

It feels good back in the box
    Lines in hand, the team all hooked,
Boys are watching on the sidelines
    Making sure nothing's overlooked.

A swing is made around the track
    They're all working as a team,
But all lathered when he gets back
    They'll need lots of work for weeks it seems.

Well, the dream is coming up once more
    To get to Calgary is the game,
If the team peaks out just right
    He could be in that four so famed.

Will they be running all as one,
    Are they fast enough this year,
Will he be lucky in the draw?
    All these thoughts he must not fear.

Are his outriders right for him
    Is the wagon in top shape
Is that lead horse really good,
    Or does he need some Bute and tape?

His thoughts not quite the same
As those of the predecessors who drive
In the ghostly dust above the track
Watching him bring his dreams alive.

They only wish they could have had
Such sponsors to support their needs
For hay and oats and back-up teams
But smile, for all things equal, they'd still lead.

So as he hooks up behind the barns
A thought flash alights as if a dove,
In the years beyond will he be there
Driving beside them in that dust above?

Will his hands be holding golden reins
Beside his heroes from the past?
He sees Lauder, Cosgrove and Hank Willard
In that dust by old Ron Glass.

They never drove for fifty thousand
But bronze cast rigs with silent teams
Still gleam in sunlight on old mantles,
A tombstone to their bygone dreams.

There in the tenseness of one brief moment
With wagons – still upon the ground,
Poised in that line up to destiny,
He waits to hear the Claxton sound.

RODEO, RODEO

I wrote this as a song, but the tune is still in my head.

Rodeo, rodeo, rodeo, rodeo
I'm goin' down the road to rodeo.
With my old pick-up and horse
And my blue heeler of course,
I'm goin' down the road to rodeo.

Oh, rodeo, rodeo, rodeo, rodeo
I'm goin' down the road to rodeo
I ain't got much jingle in my jeans
And I've been used to eatin' beans
But my horse he's had his oats most every day.

Oh, rodeo, rodeo, rodeo, rodeo
I'm goin' down the road to rodeo
I've been to Calgary, Cheyenne,
I'm on my way to Pendelton
And if my spurs stay high and loop is true
I'll be in old Los' Wages soon.

Oh, rodeo, rodeo, rodeo, rodeo
I'm goin' down the road to rodeo.

GET THAT C#*
SMELLY CAP OFFN
YOUR HEAD!
Z Z Z Z
Z
Gina ©

THE MODERN COWBOY

A few years ago Bryn Thiessen and I MC'd a talent night at Cremona and I wrote this to fit into the program.

Oh, the modern Cremona cowboy
A mere shadow of those past,
His horse is grazing freely
While his tires wear out fast.

He only wears his cowboy hat
To the Dog Pound rodeo,
And he takes along his rain cap
In case it rains or hails or snows.

You'll find him feeding cattle
In his bale handling 4-wheel pick-up,
His left hand on the power steering
While the right holds a thermal cup;

He wears a dirty crested cap
That seems glued upon his head,
And some wives have confessed
The line is drawn – when he wears it to bed.

But, as a smoothie on the dance floor
He's trying to do his part,
'Cause he's taking lessons on the latest steps
To "Achy Breaky Heart".

LEO
BROWN
RODEO
CHAMPION
Gina
©

COWBOYS ARE STILL HEROES (A TRIBUTE TO LEO BROWN)

It has been a great thrill to have this poem autographed by both Glen Hall and Leo Brown (a little tough to get Elvis P.'s autograph!). I met Glen Hall at a poetry gathering in Stony Plain where I recited this poem. Needless to say I was thrilled to meet my all time favourite hockey goalie.

On their walls back in the fifties
    Girls pinned stars of much renown,
Yes, Elvis hung on mine, and hockey's own Glen Hall
    But pinned beside them was my hero, Leo Brown.

Many stories could be told
    Of Leo's riding skills,
Of how he rode both bares and broncs
    But really mastered bulls.

I cut out all the clippings
    From any papers I could find,
And filed away all programs
    To keep facts all fresh in mind.

Leo was my hero
    But I never met him then,
Though I'd seen him ride in Calgary
    When those titles he did win.

And so it is ironic
    That when this hero I did meet,
I didn't know him without his hat
    And wearing curling shoes on his feet.

It was at the local rink,
    In Cremona to be precise,
And I asked my skip, Doug Rogers,
    "Who's that guy beside us on the ice?"

Doug looked at me and laughing
    Said, "Don't you know Leo Brown?"
I said I didn't recognize him
    With curling shoes and no hat on!

Then I told Doug he'd been my hero
    When I was just a kid,
And he said, "I'll introduce you,
    After, when we get in the pit."

Well, to me it was a thrill
    To shake my hero's hand,
Though the time had long passed
    Since his pictures, my wall spanned.

But tonight I clipped one more
    And felt real happy for you, Leo,
As I read you'd be inducted
    At the Finals Rodeo.

You'll pass through that dust ahead
    To ride abreast those famous names;
As Knight and Linder, and there with Kenny MacLean
    You'll take your place in Rodeo's Hall of Fame.

True Hunting and Camping Tales

TAGGED TROPHY

A true story that took place at a gas station in Crossfield, Alberta. Told to me by a local farmer. The art on this section page also applies to this poem.

As the rancher stood gassing up his truck
At his local service station
A truck full of beaming hunters stopped
And one asked without hesitation,

"Would you be kind enough to look
In back at our cow moose perhaps?
We don't know why upon her feet
Are nailed these iron straps!

THE FAMM CREEK GOLDEN GAUNCHE SOCIETY

Names will remain anonymous to protect the innocent!!
(But you could look up the brands). No one would own
up to the shorts with "hearts".

The mighty hunters made their camp
One late September day,
With little care they pitched their tent,
Crawled in and hit the hay.

Well, the mountain winds laughed gustily
That night near the gurgling stream
And with a mighty SWOOSH
The tent swooped down upon our hunters' dreams.

They scrambled out in snow white gaunches
And looked down upon their crumpling tent,
The moon reflected from their haunches
While over their canvas home they bent.

By the time they settled back beneath
Their fluffy eider downs,
The sun smiled as it rose up,
And the moon smiled going down!

So round the warmth of a morning campfire
With questionable sobriety,
They hilariously dubbed themselves
The Golden Gaunche Society!

Gina
©

HOBO STEW

Bagnall Park (as it's now called) is a great place to camp, (called Skunk Hollow by the locals).

They say hobos dined,
(Then happily reclined)
From the scraps a rich man would leave,

In that rusty old can
On a grey wooden stand
When found empty a hobo would grieve,

And though these old tales
Like riding the rails
Are from the thirties – a hungry decade,

I've found one that's new
I'll tell here to you
Of a more recent garbage can raid.

It seems man still craves
To relive bygone days
And a hobo's life's not been left out;

For there still are a few
Who make hobo stew
And that's what I'll tell you about.

The garbage can's not rusty
It's shiny – not dusty
As it sits over a fire made of coal;

And the water that simmers
'Neath that lid that still glimmers
Doesn't hiss on the fire through a hole.

And into this shiny pot
Is layered a lot
Of vegetables and meat for the stew.

Now all is in
This large garbage tin
And it simmers for an hour or two;

I smell carrots and cabbage
Spuds, onions and sausage,
And I'm sure a few secrets overlooked,

While the rest of us sit
The cook looks in it
And he nods that he thinks it is cooked.

His buddies jump up
To help dish it up
For they cannot wait to dig in;

And a blessing is said
For this daily bread
To be eaten from china, not tin.

Eating there in Skunk Hollow
On an evening so mellow
I pondered on what we'd all do,

If times got real dirty
Like back in the thirties
And once again we all become Bo's.

I thought with a smile
That I'd check just awhile
For the tin in George's back alley,

But if it wasn't there
I'd ride the rails out to where
I could walk to Skunk Hollow Valley.

And there I would find
An aroma of kind
I'd not smelled since dining this day.

He'd be stirring that pot
Now blackened a lot
And I hear a hiss among the coals where they lay

'Neath the ingredients in
That battered old tin
As it simmers on that hot open fire.

This time the smell hints
Of wild onions and mint
And a partridge that's been caught in a wire.

And I think that it's not
The ingredients in the pot
That are the secret of this poor man's brew,

But all of the caring
And all of the sharing
That really make good hobo stew.

HI THERE
GINA

THE BEST DEER HUNTING STORY I'VE EVER HEARD

I'd really like to meet the cop in this story sometime.

The hunter had been waiting
To get his deer last fall,
But it seemed he was unlucky
Never saw a deer at all.

The last day of the season
As he headed to the city
The time was almost midnight
But the real dark was self-pity.

Why had he not seen a deer?
How come so cursed his luck?
Why had he not found himself
A nice big four point buck?

Well, these thoughts were racing by
As he drove down the Forestry Road
When suddenly, around a bend
In the headlights something showed.

It was a deer lying on the centre line
No way to drive around it
A doe with a wounded shoulder,
She'd obviously been hit.

Well, he thought, I'll just drag her
Over to the roadside
Drive on in and call up Wildlife
They'll see she gets a ride.

Or maybe I should end her pain,
    With a bullet from my gun
But no – Wildlife would surely,
    Then put me on the run.

Why not load her in the car?
    Then she'll be cared for quick
It will save Wildlife a trip
    And I won't need my "fire stick"!

So he lay the front seat down
    And spread it with his plastic sheet
Then hauled the deer into the car
    And placed it neatly on the seat.

The seat belt wrapped around her perfect
    And snapped snugly into place;
She sat there staring with those big eyes
    And a blank look on her face.

Our hunter, smug with his decision
    Drove off – then suddenly took stock,
The unlikely thought passed through his mind,
    What if he should meet a road block?

So he avoided 1A Highway
    Took the back-roads on his drive,
Felt safe once on the city streets
    But, then, his worst fear came alive.

Right ahead – were red lights flashing,
    A road block – no escape!
What to do? He grabbed a jacket
    And wrapped it 'round her like a cape.

Then snatched a toque from off the seat
And jammed it over the doe's ears and head,
But still those big eyes blinked
And that pointy nose – too bad it wasn't red.

The cop by now was near at hand,
His light flashed in our hunter's face
So he turned his shoulder slightly forward,
Hoping he'd not flash past to second place.

But as he glanced up at the cop
And saw his eyes begin to grow,
Our hunter with e'er quick wit quipped,
"It's almost Hallowe'en you know."

The cop then asked, "Have you been drinking?"
His voice almost a dusky lisp.
"Oh, no sir, I've not had a drop,
But don't you think she's a little pissed?"

The cop said "Go, just go,
Please be on your way!"
So our hunter did as he was told
And went straight home without delay.

Now you've heard this true hunting tale,
And since I've had time to stop and think,
I've wondered if that cop went home
And poured himself a little drink?

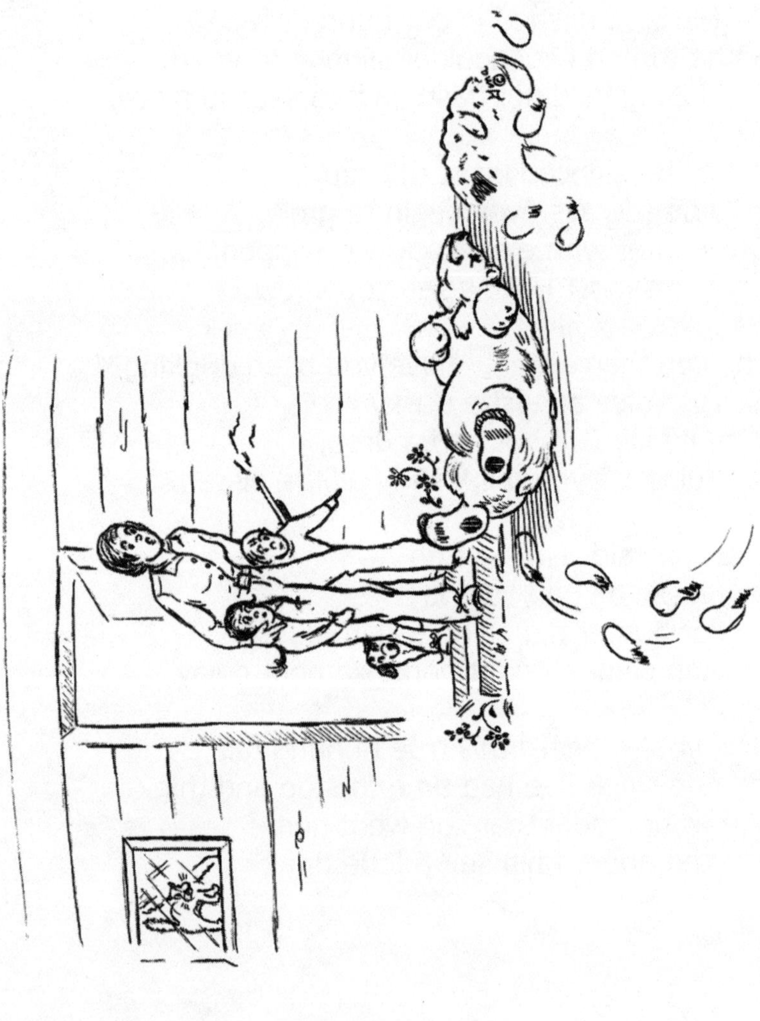

THE DAY MOTHER SHOT A BEAR

A tribute to my mother, Tillie Richards.

She was blessed with many talents
A few with you I'll share
Before I relate to you the tale
Of the day she shot a bear.

Mum could paint a landscape
With the stroke of her oil brush
Or photograph a mountain flower
Or a bird in the underbrush.

When we were young she made
All the clothes we had
From shirts, jeans and moccasins,
To those buckskin coats for Dad.

I remember when just knee high
An embroidered satin shirt she made
For Chuck Simeon to wear
To the Calgary Stampede Parade.

Her home-made brown bread
Was far and wide renowned,
But for me it was wild blueberry pie
For which she should be crowned.

Mother was a crack shot
With a Twenty-Two,
For backshot squirrels were worthless
When Simpson & Lee paid you.

She could milk a cow or stretch a wire
And packed water from the well
To wash our clothes, and sawed the wood
To heat it with as well.

She loved to pick wild berries
    When summer came along
And would ride six miles to the berry patch,
    With syrup tins hanging from the thongs.

And whether the beauty of a butterfly
    Or pulling quills from our old dog,
She taught us kids to respect
    The handiwork of God.

And at Thanksgiving time each year
    She'd take the Twenty-Two
And with us kids she'd walk the woods
    'Till we got a ruffed grouse or two.

She'd shoot them through the head
    And we'd skin them on the spot,
So why wouldn't we be proud of her
    When a bear she finally shot?

It was back there in the 60's
    When Banff had problem bears,
They'd paint their butts and tag their ears
    And truck them out of there.

Then dump them in the foothills
    And let the ranchers rant,
At these pesky Park dump bears
    Who'd never learned to hunt.

Well Mum was home alone this day
    When she heard a noise outside
And there was a scruffy blackbear
    Pawing the anthill in our yard.

The anthill beneath a poplar tree
    Was 20 yards from our front door,
And Mother anxious at a bear so close
    Thought she'd give him a little scare.

So taking Dad's 30/30 down
    She levered in a shell,
Aimed it at the bear's thick neck
    And pulled the trigger, well –

That bear dropped right where he stood
    And never moved again,
Then as Mum's luck would have it
    Our neighbour, Fred, drove in.

When Mum answered the door,
    Fred looked around to see
Who might have shot that bear
    That lay tagged beneath the tree?

The gun was resting on the door jam
    So she told her tale to Fred
And he who loved to talk and tea
    Did not linger, for he had news to spread.

We had no phones in those days,
    But with Fred the news would pass
On down the valley quickly
    Like a fire in prairie grass.

When the rest of us straggled in
    And each heard Mum tell her story,
We couldn't wait to tell our friends
    And add to her fame and glory.

But here at the time is what puzzled us
    You see she was downright mad
That we would brag her prowess up
    And on reflection I think she was sad,

That she'd shot this scruffy bear
    For her it should not be,
She'd only meant to scare him,
    Not leave him lifeless beneath the poplar tree.

MR. BEAR

A poem I wrote about a bear that frequently visited our homestead in the Peace River Country. He was sleek, shiny, cute and a pest. We named him Gentle Ben. He stole a ham out of the canner and sat at our picnic table eating pears I had left out overnight - to name only a couple of things.

Oh, Mr. Bear
Are you there
With your shiny raven hair?
I don't care,
Mr. Bear,
But please don't stand there
And stare.
Don't eat that pear,
Mr. Bear,
And stay away from there
Or you'll scare
The Old Grey Mare,
Mr. Bear.
Yes, that roast is rare,
But don't you dare!
You're not fair,
Mr. Bear.
You're such a black affair,
You should wear
A bit more flare,
Mr. Bear.
Oh, are you still there?
I do declare
You've retreated to your lair,
Mr. Bear.

There's Humour in the Telling

JUST A COYOTE

This poem is my most requested poem. Also see section picture.

What can we say of the coyote
    That has not been said before
That he is subtle, often cunning
    With a bag of tricks in store.

He dresses well, is neat and trim
    And often seeks to lure
Loners, unsuspecting, who
    Are not wise or self-assured.

He often has a bud who
    Will be there to back him up
Should he come up short himself
    When dealing with a pup.

He likes to sneak up on chickens
    Alone or in a coop,
And you should never underestimate
    Just how low he'll stoop.

Sometimes he's a loner
    But very often not
For he loves to get in bunches
    And howl when the moon is out.

Now the coyote is admired
    By many, so they say,
But would admiration last
    If they dealt with him each day?

So now you've heard about this canine
    I'm sure that you will find
You've never met a coyote
    'Till you've met the two-legged kind.

THE INVISIBLE RIDER

Sometimes kids have pretend friends.

We were riding out to the North Field
To check cattle, hay and fence
There was Dad and Doug and I, and Bob Marsh,
Whose presence made Dad a little tense.

You see, in those days we played a lot of
Cowboys and Outlaws – nothing really shady
I was always Roy Rogers,
And Doug rode as Pat Brady.

And many times Sherriff Bob Marsh
Would come and ride with us
With him along, we'd round up outlaws,
And Bob would jail them with very little fuss.

Now on this day we rode along
Right behind our Dad,
That is, Doug and I, as Pat and Roy
Talking about some outlaws we considered bad.

Then we spied Bob Marsh riding up
And both greeted him with pleasure,
Each of us moving our horses over a bit
So he could ride between at leisure.

Well, the three of us were scheming
As we rode along the trail
When Dad turned in his saddle
And gruffly told us to "cut" our little tale.

You know how kids are,
Not to be outdone
We just fell behind a little further
And continued with our fun.

But when Dad dismounted to open the gate
He darned near came unglued,
As Doug and I both hollered in unison,
"Don't shut it yet, Bob Marsh is coming through!"

SNUFF

Did you ever see a cowboy
With a bulging lower lip,
That didn't have a circle
On the pocket of his hip.

UNCLE BILL GOES TO TOWN

Mum and Dad had planned
    On going to Calgary for the day,
It was back in the early forties
    Before gravel roads and four lane highways.

Of course there were no phones
    To check when passengers were running late,
But Uncle Bill had pre-arranged to meet them,
    So they watched for him down by the gate.

Well, they waited and they waited
    So much for an early start,
But finally they spied him coming,
    And Dad gave him a little "heart to heart"!

As he thought he'd just slept in,
    But that was not the case,
Uncle Bill had got ready and hurried
    And still he lost the race,

'Cause when he got half a mile from his house
    And bent over to crawl through the fence,
He noticed he only had his long underwear on
    And he had to go back for his pants!

A SLIP OF THE LIP

Somehow his car just happened
To veer into the wide open ditch,
The young driver a bit fuzzy minded
Was not deterred by this little hitch.

As he drove home from Jasper one evening,
Thinking of the fun that he'd had,
To be sure his thoughts not contemplating
That his fun was about to turn bad.

So now as you picture this setting
And add a Mountie who comes to a stop,
You know this would not be the time
To let words from careless lips drop.

Now, as it was told to me
The young cowboy did not play it coy,
When the Mountie asked, "Are you a minor",
He slurred "No, I'm just a cowboy".

Wanting to know what the Mountie did then
My informant finished his tale,
"Why the cowboy slept out the rest of the night
In the warmth of the Mountie's fine jail!"

WAGON TRACKS

Everyday conversation can often have a twist.

"Hi, Wagon Tracks,
It's 'Fat Joe' here,
Give me a call back
So I can bend your keen ear".

The phone cracks down
Wagon Tracks says, "Fat chance
He has I'll call back,
Just to hear what he wants.

It could be the tractor
Or maybe the plow
Or is it the calf cradle
That he's after right now."

You see, 'Fat Joe'
Wants her to call back, and be nice,
'Cause for her long distance is free
On that special line price.

But 'Wagon Tracks' is not anxious
To call back 'Fat Joe'
On her monthly nickel
When it's well that she knows,

He likely wants to borrow,
A machine or a tool
To use a bit 'freely'
While playing it 'cool'.

And besides the insult
Of being called 'Wagon Tracks'
Really shows up 'Fat Joe'
For the couth that he lacks,

For it's a slight to the Lady
He's called up just now
'Cause he's referring to the lines
On her face and her brow!

THE 6X HAT

There is even more to this story, but I'll tell you another time.
**The higher the X's the better the quality of cowboy hats.*

The suave distinguished gentleman
With "cowboy" in his heart
Strode up to the "Black Hat" booth
At the Houston Livestock Mart.

The Stetsons all arranged so neatly
Were set off even more
By the tall, fair, shapely Texas beauty
Who completed the décor.

Our gentleman began to barter
With the lady fair and slim
As she described her 4X hats, and that,
She had a black one just for him.

Now our gentleman said to the lady,
"I really must confess,
A black 6X* is what I want,
But at 4X price or less."

Then she soothed in her Texas drawl,
"I don't have a 6X on hand for you
But come back and see me later and,
I'll see what I can do."

When he strode back that evening
She smiled and reached within her store
For a bag from which she pulled the hat,
That he'd been waiting for.

He bent forward and she fit it
    On his head so perfectly
And at that moment he saw no X's
    But a curvaceous "V".

He paid the lady 4X price
    And returning to the crew
Said to one, "Come with me and I'll deal
    On a 6X hat for you."

"First, let me feel that new hat",
    So he placed it in her hand
And when she rolled it over
    (For all to see) was 4X on the band!

Well, I think I'll hire that sales lady
    And see if she can sell – ahem!
My one-eyed horse and foot rot cow,
    And get 6X price for them.

Gina ©

HOME SWEET HOME
SHHH

SILENT NIGHT

Jim and his close neighbour Richard
While tipping a few one night
Didn't see the hours slip past
'Till the bar doors closed up tight.

Not so inept as they seemed,
They left their cars on the street,
Hailed a taxi – then worried,
About the happy wives they'd meet.

Well, Jim got dropped off first,
Snuck in through his garage,
Quietly fumbled his way through the door
Then stopped – awaiting the barrage.

So far, so good – not a sound did he hear,
And took off his shoes in the dark
Then crawled down the hall on hands and knees,
To avoid a noisy spark.

Finally, at the bathroom he fumbled
Out of his smoky clothes,
Then tiptoed into the bedroom –
Still no sound arose.

Quietly, he snuck to the bed;
Gently lifting the covers and slid –
Between the sheets so gently,
And closed his bleary eyelids.

He breathed slowly a moment and waited,
Expecting a stir and a blast
But nothing – and drifted off thinking –
"I've fooled that woman at last!!"

Next morning his dear wife queried,
"What time were you in last night?"
"Oh", he said, "About 11 o'clock."
(He thought) No sense in starting a fight!

"That's funny, it was well past one",
And she gave a little cough,
"You see, I was at Richard's when he got home,
And he told us they'd just dropped you off!"

Family & Friends at the End of a Dream

TIME TO THINK

Give me some peace and quiet,
Give me some time to think,
The kids are under my feet
The dishes are piled in the sink;
The dog's barking from the step full bore
The old man's lying on the living room rug
I can't hear above his snores;
But an idea just crossed my mind,
I should have thought of it before,
Give me my boots and saddle,
I'll go out and climb on my horse.

THE CHICKEN DANCERS

The Richards Brothers were raised on and near the Stoney Indian Reserve and learned many of their customs. Gina told me this story as she was there.

Audley, Ed, Jim and Bill
The Richards' Boys by name
And even though their blood ran white
They chicken danced just the same.

No house party or local dance
Was ever quite complete
Until someone brought out the wash tub
And The Boys danced to the Tom-tom's beat.

And so the story of one chicken dance
Still lingers in the minds of some,
And though The Boys now ride the great divide
Memory, still hears their song and drum.

After a long day trailing cattle
From the Bar C to the train
Waiting on the tracks at Morley,
The Boys would dance to their refrain.

No, not in a dance hall or in a house
Or even in the Morley Store,
But up on top of an empty boxcar
They chicken danced these brothers four.

The Stoneys gathered 'round to watch them
Along with others from the drive
Laughed, and slapped their buckskin leggings
While white brothers brought their dance alive.

And so, as these words flow from my pen,
    And I preserve this story told to me of them,
I still hear my Dad sing and beat that Tom-tom
    For you see he was the one named Jim.

CUSTER'S SECOND CHANCE

Marvin could double for General George Custer anywhere.
He had been through a series of mishaps when I wrote
this poem for a benefit they had for him and his family.

His hair so long and flowing,
    Blond and shoulder length,
Enhanced by his full droop moustache
    Giving the appearance of strength.

I thought of that General who led
    The battle of the Little Big Horn,
And how me met his death
    On that fateful afternoon.

How the Red Man took his scalp
    And counted it a mighty coup,
Yet, here I sat having coffee with the General,
    And I couldn't see one Sioux.

He'd walked in through the door
    "Meet Marvin", my husband said,
But all I could think of was Custer
    And that he really wasn't dead.

Now "Custer", I know your shoulder's right bad
    And your leg's all dressed up in white,
That most everything you do is an irritation,
    But let me leave you with this bit of insight,

Those who believe in reincarnation
    Say each life improves on its stair;
So you must be filled with pure optimism,
    For no Tomahawk has passed through your hair.

TO THE BUCKLE MAN

South California's call has beckoned,
    It's the warmer clime I've reckoned
That calls you back to that hazy shroud
    Of red hot sand, and sky without a cloud.

But won't you miss the clear blue mountains
    And the rushing ice water fountains,
And the crisp, fresh morning air
    When you step away from hyar?

Oh, I think you will, no doubt,
    But that's what life is all about
'Cause nothing ever stays the same
    In this quest for gain and fame.

But as the physical roots are shook
    When a time to move's been took,
There will always be those ties
    Never seen at all by eyes.

For friendship's tentacle is not pulled
    Nor by miles or money ruled
Like a winning buckle highly polished,
    It travels with you – ever cherished.

A FRIEND – BIG FARMER BIG

A tribute written for Leonard Kininmonth's funeral.

It's hard to say good-bye
    To a long time friend you've known
But you know where they have passed
    Some good trails will be showing.

I know each one of you
    Has his favourite thoughts of Len
But the one I'm going to share
    Will reach way back when,

Leonard came to visit us
    Way back up on the Ghost
He knew my Dad quite well because –
    He bought Leonard's oats.

But Doug and I had never seen him
    And when he walked in through the door
Our eyes grew wide, and mouths dropped open –
    We'd seen this man before!

You see, Doug had a little book
    With a farmer on the front
That looked so much like Leonard,
    We thought it was a stunt.

The farmer in this children's book
    Was very large of frame
And so "Big Farmer Big"
    Is what the book was named.

This man had hands of stature
    That could hold a dozen eggs
And his eyes so very blue
    From the pages they would gaze.

He had a winning smile that
    Reached from ear to ear
And from the pages of this book
    A hearty laughter you could hear.

And now I've told you of this story
    I hope that you will dig
Why our nickname for Leonard
    Was always "Big Farmer Big".

A TRIBUTE TO JOE KLEINER

We'll miss you at Dog Pound next year
Where we'd visit and tell a few stories,
Your smile, your handshake, your hug
Are now but a fond memory,

But it didn't seem to matter at all
That I didn't know you as long as some
Even at that first rainy show where we met
There you kept my kids dry in your home.

You introduced me to Doug and Joanne,
And while cracking me open a brew
You said, "meet Jim and Jay,
Right now that's it for this crew.

Well, it rained hard that year at Dog Pound
And we all piled in your motorhome,
I remember the crew sitting 'round your table
While I spouted some cowboy poems.

At least eight years have passed since that day
And each year we all look for our seating;
Mostly we've not seen each other since last year,
And look forward to our annual meeting.

Well, at Dog Pound next year there'll be sadness
The old crew will gather again
But there'll be a space by the fence we well know
Which in our minds will still bear your name.

We may be feeling a bit heavy at heart
    When a breeze will turn into a whirlwind
And come dancing right over among us
    To pick us up and bring back to mind,

That the last thing you'd want was us sorrowing
    You'd wish us to laugh and have fun
Your voice in the wind, no quiet whisper shouts,
    "C'mon, cheer, I made a hell of a ride to 81"!

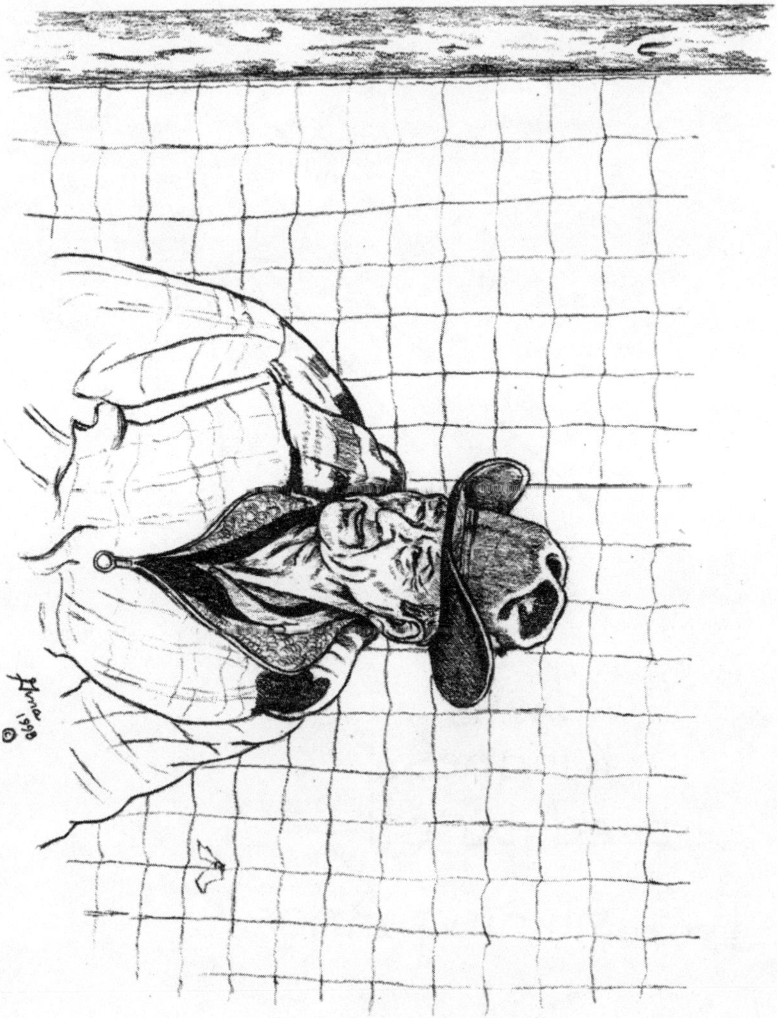

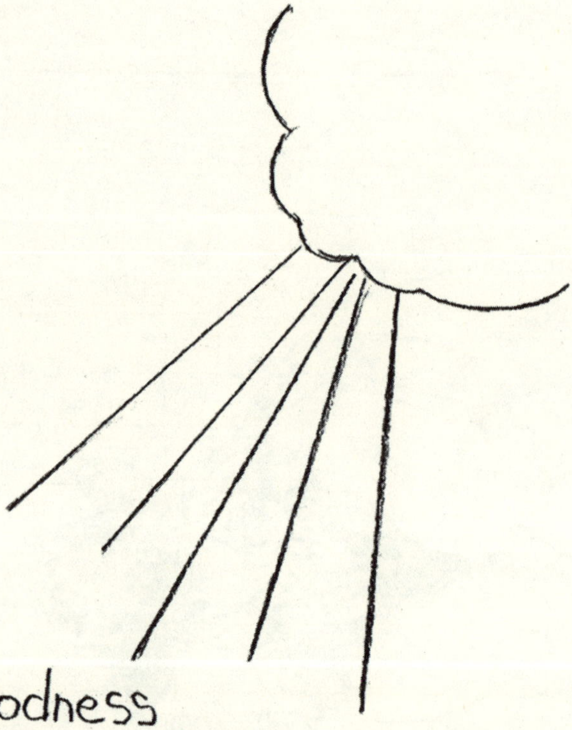

Goodness
Kindness
Loved by all
Two Shining Angels

Gina ©

TRIBUTE TO JAYE & YVONNE BOWLEN

This poem came after I attended the funeral of our neighbours and friends (descendants of early Alberta pioneers), following their tragic murder.

They are here – the descendants of the pioneers
Paying respect, feeling anger expressing their grief
Not sure how to deal with the shock and reality,
Looking for comfort, giving comfort, finding relief.

They're all here, the families from our history books,
Sitting in the oak pews of St. Mary's Cathedral
And I saw the backdrop – like a mural weathered in time,
Saw the faces, their names in my mind as if written on the wall.

It could have been one hundred years ago, or more,
The Stetsons held in the hands of neighbours and friends,
The redman with tears in his eyes, the redcoat out of uniform,
Silence when we heard the voice of Black Robe's descendent.

I thought, "This is a gathering of our history, this is history",
And as the follower of Black Robe spoke his words
You could feel the healing flow of the Creator's Spirit,
And the descendants of the pioneers still knew He was Lord.

REMINISCING WITH BOBBY AND SUNNI

Written for their 40th Wedding Anniversary, 10 years ago, I changed it to 50th as we celebrated it in July , 2003.

From fifty years we can select
A tale or two about these folks
Who tonight are the elect
Of my creative pen's poetic strokes.

It seems its ink just pours out
To get down those little incidents
That your friends might freely spout
Without a thought of hesitance.

Before they met there's lots to say,
Like Bobby's race to get to school,
He'd mount old Tiko each school day,
Six miles in 20 minutes, was his rule.

No, his teachers did not mark at all
For conditioning horses to meet the bell,
But it did not escape the eyes of Dingwall
Whose wagon rolled on that Half Mile of Hell.

Now, Sunni came from Buffalo,
Only a dot on the shortgrass land,
She came to find a man you know
While teaching school at old Lochend.

Now Sunni's favourite colour, RED
She waved aplenty at old Bobby Bull,
And soon we know that they were wed
In the heat of August when it's not cool.

They honeymooned within a tent
Not strange for a trophy hunter's wish,
Though it seemed odd no horses went...
But then, they say, you went to fish!

You set right in and ran your dairy
Which you "squeezed" your living from
And Bobby's vision grew somewhat bleary,
Though along the way five sons were born.

There were those days when Bobby's truck
Used the ditch for its main road,
There you might find him stuck,
'Cause 'twas not the truck that packed a load.

Now down the years Bobby finally built his dream
To sell the cows and pack up his rifle and tent,
And along with his good friend Carl it seems
We're not sure whether with bullets or tales the woods
were rent.

Or maybe while Carl or Bobby sat around
The campfire trying to outdo each others wit,
Sunni took her rifle and a trophy found,
While those story tellers would take and embellish it.

Now we all know Sunni has her passions
For exotic clothes and digging up old bones,
But I think those fancy fashions
Are for that Old Fossil – the one not made of stone.

I know we could tell stories all the night
That would leave you rolling out there on the grass
And to congratulate you Bobby and Sunni is our
delight,
'Cause you've hung in there while 50 years have
passed.

OVER 50 CLUB

Gordon Murphy - Inducted July 22, 1997

(Sorry – this isn't a "Hall of Fame" – just a dusty old corral on a hot summer's day!)

For a good friend.

"Dues – Paid in Full"
The gate sign reads,
With a half century of living
You've gained entrance indeed!

'Cause now with timidity
Like a "wildy" will do,
You've snuck through the gate
To lick salt with the crew.

So now that you're "in"
You won't feel left "out".
When the rest of us 50's
We laugh and we shout.

Now you're most welcome
'Cause you've "come of age"
So we'll share some club "secrets"
(They could fill a page),

Like – It matters not
If your hair is real thin
Or if the roll at your belt
Is like a big double chin,

Or if you've lost just a touch
Of the spring in your step,
And to read this poem
Your spectacles help;

Or when the clock strikes four
You're not sneaking in from the bar,
No – you just wonder
Why the bathroom's so far!!

And on top of all this
Your memory's spent,
When you get where you're going
You forgot why you went,

So now that you're FIFTY
And I've built up your morale –
Swing shut the gate boys
We've got him corralled!

HONEYMOON WARNING

Remember those days with Ed, Doug and John,
How you'd all get ready and your hunting clothes don?
And I can still hear Doug and Eddy's low groans
"If Wasson's not ready, we'll go it alone".

For while the rest of the boys loaded all of the gear
John would be combing his hair in front of the mirror,
And I could never see why this was of much use
When all they'd be chasing were ugly old moose.

At last to the mountains they finally fled
With horses and packs and an old wagon bed.
Now the rest of this story is strictly hearsay,
But then isn't that the way of most of our history?

Well, I don't recall if any moose were shot
But there are a few tales I never forgot
About how John, for this two day hunting trip
Went all modern with a pillow and slip.

But that's not all, for I heard them exclaim
"For two days he needs all that shaving cream?"
"And ten pairs of socks and two pair of clean shorts,
Must be insurance if a bull moose should snort"!

Well, Donna you're probably wondering by now
What this has to do with a wedding and vows
Well, what I've really tried to say is simply that,
For a weekend honeymoon John will need two days
to pack!

FALL WOOD ROAD

My only free verse poem.

I drove down that long, brown snaking wood road,
Winding among the leafless willows, poplars and
conifers,
Bare looking, with the dried faded grasses
Bending their heads over its black edges.

No longer smooth with warm dust flying,
But rough and bumpy with frozen mud ridges,
I noticed places blotched white with skiffs of snow
Because the sun had not found its way through the
overhanging spruce.

And there were stories left there by the forest folk
In the frozen ridges and in the snowy patches.
I saw them there when I stopped and searched the
hardened ground
And glanced upon the frosty snow.

I'd cut the motor, and though I could barely hear a
sound
They'd been there for I saw the long splayed toes of
the moose track
Cemented in the soft road shoulder, and the
Dainty tracks of Mr. Meadow Mouse patterned in the
snow.

I looked ahead at the bends, the dips, and the
hollows, winding to the end
And momentarily listened to the rustle of the dead
grasses and dry clicking branches
Moved only by the chill north breeze, then with a
shiver, I turned
Toward the warmth of my car, and quickly motored
through that fall wood road.

THE PALOMINO FILLY

A Metaphoric Poem dedicated to the blond, attractive, talented Casey Peden, as penned at a Pincher Creek Poetry Gathering.

The fiddle music danced its love song
On the warm night breeze of June,
The strands of "Faded Love" wailed rich
'Neath the fullness of the moon.

There a Bachelor Band* milled restless
Near the banks of Pincher Creek
The music, moon, the warmth of June
Caused blood to race 'neath hides so sleek.

They saw her enter stepping lightly
The moonbeams shone on her golden mane
Her slender body flowed in rhythm
To the fiddle strings' refrain.

The Bachelor Band put on alert
By this gentle filly's presence
Watched as she stepped upon the platform,
Her youthful voice pulling at their essence.

I sat there watching quietly
And when she finished her melody of song,
She made her way up to the Hill above,
The Bachelor Band – following close along.

All but one, that was tied by MC obligations
Pawing at the Mike right here on stage;
Impatient with the long line up of poets
Each waiting to recite at least a page.

Oh, that Bachelor left behind
    Tried so hard to close the poets soon!
'Cause he could hear those love songs on the fiddle,
    Knowing others danced that filly to their tunes.

The evening finally ended,
    I don't remember when,
And thoughts of the Palomino Filly,
    And Bachelor Band – left my mind right then.

But a few weeks later
    I spotted them, out on a Stony Plain
The Bachelor Band – loosely scattered,
    Each nonchalantly looking for the filly once again.

Then I saw her – stepping oh so lightly
    And one by one – so did the Bachelor Band,
But woe to them for she strolled along,
    A tall, dark stranger holding her gentle hand.

I glanced, and soon those lonely bachelors
    Regrouped as of old into their tight knit band
Outwardly the Palomino Filly
    No longer appeared to penetrate their stand.

** In the wild, Bachelor Bands are usually made up of young stud horses that have not the size or strength to steal mares for themselves from an older more powerful stud's band. Geldings will sometimes hang out with these young studs as well.*

THE SPURS

I snapped the bull whip
Not with finesse or grace,
But it did snap I remember,
A satisfied grin on my face.

Now I could show off a bit
And snap it in front of others
Although when you're only 10
There were still some ground rules from mother.

This bull whip was given to me
By an oldtimer from Maple Creek by chance,
His name was Barney Lindner
And he'd come to Alberta to ranch.

He bought the best ranch in the valley
He knew just what to look for,
Open hills, running water, high grass
And he raised the best Hereford cattle, I've ever
seen since or before.

My Dad hayed for him every summer,
They built huge stacks from pure prairie wool,
And with horses and sweeps and wood stackers,
No tractors or balers for tools.

Tourists would stop on old 1A Highway
And take pictures of these huge stacks of hay,
Built like giant loaves of bread,
They're still pictured in my mind to this day.

Now Billy Linder joined Barney at Two Rivers
And they were friends of my family for years;
When they sold their ranch and moved back to Maple,
We were all darned close to tears.

The last time we stopped they were packing
And I'd just sold my big 4-H calf in town;
We'd come to pay Barney what I owed him,
But he said, "Wait, 'til the next time you're down".

Then Billy took me aside and he gave me
An old set of spurs that he had,
Said they'd belonged to a man long dead
And he didn't want to pack them too bad.

The rowels were blunted and worn,
There's almost a half inch of play,
The straps all worn and stiff,
Had certainly seen better days.

Well, I never saw Barney or Billy again
And the bull whip is long worn out and old,
But I still have those spurs with the silver leaf trim
That's underlaid beneath by pure gold.

SEPTEMBER

September - the blooming month of colour
A soft and glorious array of wraps,
Draped eloquently across the countryside
Preparing summer for her siege of winter naps.

Oh, the splendrous array that stretches wide
Does not appear in any other time of year,
And slowly fades away into October and November
To await the birth of winter's white career.

Come and gather here upon the golden hill
With rust tinged edges and greenish undergrowth
That spreads as far as yon purpled range of
mountains,
And melts down into the valley's green velvet
trough.

A majestic scene filling the soul with serenity,
With calm and thoughtful eye one seeks to
remember
That not every day and month brings fulfilling
peacefulness
As the colour-laden hours of ripe September.

THE DREAM

In memory of Wilma McIntosh

The crocus blooms
The meadowlark sings
On the coulee's edge
Where her mind takes wings.

The prairie wool's sweetness
Lifts up on the breeze
Filling her senses
While kids play at her knees.

Like pups by a den
They frolic and scheme
But they cannot erase
The thoughts of her dream;

The prairie's the stage
With its great sweeping arc
And she sees herself singing
With the voice of the lark.

But unfulfilled dreams
Are a code of the West
And accompany the dreamer
To her final rest.

The stage is still there
The crocus is blooming,
Hear the lark's melody
On the breeze, still free roaming?

And the threads of her dream
Are found on the wind
Left there for another
With likeness of mind.

Her dream now a poem
In these thoughts for a friend,
Like the West we all love,
The Dream never ends.

* * * * *

We hope you enjoyed the ride.

Wendy & Gina

About The Illustrator

Gina McDougall-Cohoe is one of Canada's most talented and well known sculptors of Western themed bronze art. She grew up on The Bar C Ranch on the north side of the Ghost River, across from the author's family.

An excellent horse trainer, Canadian Champion Barrel Racer, as well as superb sketch artist, Gina has first hand knowledge of her subjects. Her sketches, often spiced with humour, are a delight to view.

Recipients of Gina's bronze sculptures have included the Queen of England and many of the cowboy champions at the Calgary Stampede.

Gina's works keep the Spirit of the West alive. You will delight in her thoughtful sketches that illustrate Wendy's cowboy poetry.

About The Author

Wendy (Richards) Vaughan was born in 1943, and spent her entire growing up years on the family cattle and horse ranch 30 miles west of Cochrane, Alberta.

In 1966 she married Walter Vaughan. Following four years in the mid-1970's "proving" their homesteads in the Peace River country, they returned to the family farm north of Cochrane, where they raised two daughters.

Never without a horse (or 10), and a small herd of commercial Hereford cattle, Wendy has kept close to her roots.

She became enthused about cowboy poetry after attending a Baxter Black evening in 1988. He encouraged her to attend the first Pincher Creek Poetry Gathering that year.

Wendy says, "I only had four poems for that first Gathering, and was nervous. In poetry you are revealing yourself. But when I saw tears in the eyes of old ranchers and heard them laugh, all in the same poem, I knew my poetic stories rang true."